TYRONE E. BUSH

KNOW L.I.E.S.

UNDERSTANDING LIFE, INVESTMENTS, ENTREPRENEURSHIP, AND SUCCESS

KNOW L.I.E.S.

UNDERSTANDING LIFE, INVESTMENTS, ENTREPRENEURSHIP, AND SUCCESS

TYRONE E. BUSH

Copyright © 2020 by Tyrone E. Bush

All rights reserved. This book is protected by the copyright laws of the United States of America. No portion of this book may be reproduced, stored in a retrieval system, or transmitted in any form or by any means–electronic, mechanical, photocopy, recording, scanning, or other–except for brief quotations in critical reviews or articles, without the prior written permission of the publisher.

Published in North Augusta, South Carolina by Tyrone E. Bush

Unless otherwise identified, Scripture quotations are taken from the King James Version (public domain).

Scripture quotations noted NIV are from THE NEW INTERNATIONAL VERSION®, Copyright © 1973, 1978, 1984 International Bible Society. Used by permission of Zondervan.

ISBN: 978-1-09836-218-8 (softcover)

ISBN: 978-1-09836-219-5 (eBook)

To my beautiful wife, Veleta, the love of my life who has walked every step of the journey through *Know L.I.E.S.* Thank you for the sacrifices, understanding, and undying love you have given.

To my children, Jayla and Paris, each day I live, it is my desire to create and leave a legacy for each of you. You all are my greatest assets!

To the phenomenal people across the world that will read this book, thank you for allowing me to share my story and the information I've gained along the way. You have chosen to value the asset of you above material assets, step into the unknown, and face your fears head-on. As you live your best life, the money will come.

Contents

Preface 1

Introduction 5

Your First Asset 9

Applied Knowledge is Power 19

The Credit Card Craze 27

Bad Debt or Investment? 35

The Door to Entrepreneurship 43

Love Life. Make Money 53

Preface

Before we get into the meat and potatoes of this book, allow me to clear up any misconceptions or overarching expectations. First of all, I am not a financial expert, guru, or wizard. I cannot spew out financial formulas, investments, or business ideas that will make you well-off by tomorrow or next week. Neither will you find an economic degree or most of the letters from the alphabet following my name. This book will not be the only book beneficial to understanding the world of financial stability, wealth, or investments. This book's premise is to tell my story and start you on the path to changing your mindset concerning financial wealth. Inside this book, I will provide useful information and tools to help you begin your monetary journey. It may not be the "perfect" fit for you, but it will move you into a place of thinking from a different perspective. Shifting your mindset or perspective on how you view financial freedom is the first step. Through my personal testimony, I will illustrate that your portfolio of assets, investments, and business ideas can change when you change your mindset toward finances.

In as much as I am not a financial guru, neither am I a minister. This is not a spiritual book that will overwhelm you with a plethora of scriptures concerning money. Still, in my study and research, I have found a few verses in the Bible that pertain to the subject at hand. To begin with, 1 Timothy 6:10a is a verse that is often quoted. This verse is mentioned by those who do not possess enormous amounts of money. They have attempted to use it as validation for why they do not need or desire more money. Unfortunately, the verse is usually quoted out of context. It is actually written, "The *love* of money is a root of all kinds of evil" (italics added). Not only will you find that verse concerning money in the Bible, but you will also find several others. The previous and subsequent scriptures are only mentioned to make a point concerning how we think about money. Ecclesiastes 3:10c (New International Version [NIV]) states, "...and money is the answer for everything." Before you agree with those words, please note there are additional words to the verse. Unfortunately, some people believe money *is* the answer to everything. Well, money is definitely the answer to several things, but not everything. Whether you are wealthy or poor, money cannot answer everything that happens in life. Money is a necessary asset. Even so, money cannot demonstrate how to love your spouse, heal a disease, or deal with the heartbreaking grief which comes after a loved one passes away. Yes, money is essential and has its place in our lives, but it is *not* the answer to everything.

Although I did not attain the financial training that many financial masterminds and authors possess, since I was a child, I have been interested in the world of finance. Growing up as the youngest of seven siblings in the small town of Aiken, South Carolina, my family did not have an abundance of wealth. With eight children to take care of, I don't even recall a time where we ever had an abundance of money to spend. Yes, we had what we needed, but our wants were not a priority. Living in scarcity and trying to provide for children was quite overwhelming for my mother. Still, she never complained. She did the best she could. My mother kept a full-time job and worked additional side jobs, such as cleaning houses, to make sure she provided for her family. My mother did not have a college degree. Yet, she instilled in us values such as hard work, independence, and respect that would benefit us throughout our lives, and she gave us skills that would help us succeed in the world.

Over the years, I watched how hard my mother worked to take care of her family, and from watching her, I knew that hard work would be one of the most valuable assets of my life. With a ten-year gap between my next-to-the-youngest sibling and me, I was the only child still left at home once my siblings became of age to leave the nest. Throughout my time at home, my mother continued to teach me valuable lessons. One nugget of wisdom was the art of being resourceful. According to my mother, it was never enough to imagine what I could be; it was equally important to know and use the skills within me. As a young boy, I always wanted to learn. Besides learning through school, I gained a great deal of knowledge from a set of encyclopedias. Some of you may be quite familiar with the door-to-door encyclopedia salesmen. Wow, the memories. The days of hearing a knock on the door and listening to the speech about how we needed these books is a treasured memory. Using an encyclopedia took longer than using the search engines of the twenty-first century. One search could require you to look through several books! Our younger generation will never come close to knowing that experience. They have been introduced and become accustomed to the world of Google™ since birth, where it takes about two seconds to find information on any subject!

Nonetheless, I grew up searching for information through encyclopedias with the first letter of the subject I wanted to study. The information in these books would captivate me for hours. The majority of the time, the encyclopedia that began with the letter "E" for economics was what I chose. For some reason, economics was usually the subject that often caught my attention. Back in this day and age, we didn't have the fancy names that are now used in the financial field, such as *assets, investments, entrepreneurship,* or should I say, I wasn't aware of those terms. In high school, we studied economics, which taught us how to handle money. The class was not as in-depth as the college courses or financial workshops are now. Each course was simple, yet I learned enough to help me understand money, especially for the amount my family had. I always knew that I did not want to become an adult and continue to struggle financially. Perhaps, I just wanted to, one day, experience living a stable life while being able to afford all of my needs and some of my wants. I desired more, not for the sake of just having more but to experience the freedom that being financially secure could provide.

Before writing this book, I wanted to be wealthy and have a boatload of assets in my investment portfolio. No, I have not hit the "I'm rich" buzzer yet; however, reaching that goal is not a foreign concept. And I am on the right path! Wealth and riches do not come overnight, but the harder you work in the present, the less you'll have to worry in the future. Throughout this book, you will read illustrations of my willingness, determination, and sacrifice to focus my attention on achieving financial freedom. Facing some tough decisions and making tremendous sacrifices was, at times, daunting. Yet, with my goal at the forefront, I have made huge strides. Often, we do not achieve our goals because we fail to face the truth of what we need to change. We must remember that we cannot fix what we do not face.

Introduction

"Money, money money, money, money. Some people got to have it. Some people really need it." —The O'Jays

The words the O'Jays sang are still influential to this day. It is beneficial to have money, but it is also helpful to have the right state of mind when you possess it. Acquiring cash, investments, stocks, or property is a great accomplishment. However, those assets are no good if your mindset is incapable of handling all that comes with maintaining those assets. As I stated in the preface, I do not possess a degree in finance or economics, but I have focused my mind on gaining knowledge and creating wealth for my family.

No, I am not going to write about any Ponzi schemes or multi-level marketing. If you choose to increase your assets or build your business by utilizing those methods, that will be your choice. Speaking of choice, each of us must make them in every area of our lives. Our choices can either lead us down the road to success or failure. Although opinions or research may give us the wisdom we seek, we can choose to use or ignore the information. A financial broker cannot "make" you invest in stocks. Even though they share investment options, if they are not appealing to your portfolio, then you have the right to say "no" to those investments. The ability to choose is powerful, but it is imperative to choose wisely.

Throughout this book, you will read about some of my personal decisions… the good and the bad. Of course, financial experts such as Robert Kiyosaki and Dave Ramsey have written books that delved into the meat and potatoes of finances and investments. They have also shared their successes and failures. Even financial experts, such as the ones listed, do not always make the right choices. However, what sets them apart is persistence. Reaching your business goals or obtaining assets and investments is not a one-time transaction. Investing in stocks and bonds or buying property requires taking chances, being persistent, and learning from each experience. Unfortunately, we look at failure as a loss, but I disagree. We should view it as a learning experience. After a successful or unsuccessful moment, ask yourself these questions and answer them honestly:

1. What did I learn from this experience?
2. What can be done differently?
3. Did I weigh all the options?
4. Is more research required?
5. If it was an unfortunate event, can I pick myself up and try again?

Yes, these are simple questions. The answers you give will help create a stable mindset when pursuing your passion or dream of becoming a business owner or investor. You cannot give up at the first instance of an unsuccessful choice. Achieving your financial goals requires a steady state of mind.

In each chapter, I share my personal achievements and obstacles with complete transparency. My hope is that you can develop your own story, achieve your goals, and create a legacy of wealth for you and your family. No, it is not going to be easy, and persistence is essential. Knowing your heart's desire toward achieving financial freedom or delving into entrepreneurship is crucial. Why? Because it determines how hard you are willing to work and what you are ready to sacrifice to achieve your goals. It is not about comparing yourself to others because you must run the race that is set before you and follow your own path. Whatever pitfalls you face and whatever successes you experience are just for you!

At some point, we all have been faced with how we view ourselves and how we view those who we believe are successful. Our thought process concerning reaching the place that we consider successful can be overwhelming.

INTRODUCTION

Achieving the goals of clearing credit card debt, paying off good and bad debt, or becoming an entrepreneur, in the beginning, can be quite terrifying. None of those are accomplished quickly, and each requires a great deal of determination, patience, hard work, and even a little faith. Our desire is to get to the finish line. We want to enjoy the perks that come with clearing debt or starting our own business. But, first, we must walk through the process. The process involves changing our mindset, research, college courses (if needed), joining networking groups, and making sacrifices. We cannot afford to have the same attitude toward spending when we desire to move forward in achieving our financial ambitions. Our minds must be focused on our target.

Delayed gratification has to come into play during this journey. The "I want it now" mentality has to take a backseat or be completely demolished from your thinking. Sure, you can enjoy life. But it may be necessary to slightly scale back (especially monetarily) until you have met or exceeded your goal. What do I mean by this? I mean, you simply cannot get close to your goal and not finish. You must maintain a mindset to save, clear debt, or open your business. It is ludicrous to get close and stop doing the work because something did not go as you expected. For example, it is uncommon for a cross-country runner to get close to the finish line but never meet the goal of crossing over it. No matter whether the runner is in first or last place, each runner crosses the finish line. No one runs to the sideline and becomes a spectator just because they are not in first place. In like fashion, you will never attain your goal of crossing over to becoming financially secure if you choose to spend money before you make money. Your goal should never be to start strong as a participant, just to end up sitting the race out as a spectator, watching everyone else cross over into the land of financial success.

My main focus is to share the mental, physical, emotional, and financial processes I applied in my walk toward economic security. There have and will continue to be many successes and failures, and sometimes, life brings circumstances that happen unexpectedly. But with each step, there is a determination that I have set in my heart. Although you are reading my story, you should begin to write your own story. Writing your own story will help you recognize your tenacity and drive you toward realizing your dreams. I want to ensure that you understand the peaks and valleys of achieving financial stability, acquiring assets, or becoming an entrepreneur. I hope you will think about your vision, your family, and, most importantly…YOURSELF! You are a valuable asset. Once you realize your importance, reaching the goal you have set will not be an unnerving task but an amazing victory.

Your First Asset

Your first asset is not about whether you have wealth or have discovered the perfect investment to make money while you sleep. Simply put, it is about transformational thinking concerning how you see *your* worth. It is about living an enriched life, whether you have more than enough, just enough, or barely enough. Unfortunately, we do not always take an opportunity to explore who we genuinely are. Before we purchase tangible assets, we research the market, read the background information, and check out resources before making the final decision to purchase. In the same manner, we should be spending time getting to know ourselves, checking out our inner resources, and understanding who we were created to be. We cannot fulfill who we were created to be unless we spend time examining who we are, and who we are should not be defined by what we have.

Time and again, when we talk about assets, we *only* discuss finances, businesses, and investments. According to Dictionary.com, an asset is not only property or possessions owned by a person, but it is also defined as "a useful or valuable thing, person, or quality." Sadly, acquiring financial assets has become more important than recognizing that there is a more excellent asset than money, property, or stocks. Our desire to obtain financial stability at whatever cost can make us lose focus on our most significant assets. Perhaps, society has pressured us to focus solely on material things. Sometimes, we focus on material things until we believe that they will merge us into a higher status or cause us to be recognized by a prominent group of people. We have become overly inundated by how people on the outside view us. Perhaps, we have become so accustomed to our lavish lifestyle that we almost sell our souls to ensure we keep it. There is nothing wrong with achieving a certain financial status; that is one reason it was important for me to eliminate unnecessary debt. If our mindset is not focused on the key assets, then once we obtain material assets, we will not fully experience the value of living an enriched life, so before we delve into a financial asset state of mind concerning wealth, investments, or entrepreneurship, we must talk about the most critical asset…YOU! Your life and the lives of your family are the most significant assets.

Have you ever taken an opportunity to evaluate who you are from your own perspective? I'm not talking about what others say about you or how they view you. I'm talking about what you say about yourself and how you view yourself. So what do you say? How do you view yourself? What valuation would you give yourself? Take a moment to think about it. Can we be honest? It is often difficult for us to answer these questions without considering the things we possess. For far too long, we have been identified by what we have tangibly, not by what we have inside our souls, hearts, and minds. To have a real asset state of mind, we must first know how valuable we are, regardless of what we have or don't have. Our worth should not be measured by the amount of money, property, or investments we have obtained. The amounts we see on our bank statements or in our money market accounts should not define who we are as a person. It should be measured by our innermost thoughts and the way we treat ourselves and others, as well as our level of integrity and loyalty.

In life, we experience situations and circumstances that can cause us to stand on the highest mountaintop or crouch in the lowest part of the valley. These peaks and valleys do not necessarily define who we are, nor do they unequivocally identify our family life. Each situation we face can be a defining moment, not the definition for an entire lifetime. We mustn't get caught in the web of attaining things and not maintaining our most prominent asset. Our lives' ultimate premise should be love for ourselves and our family, not the economic assets or businesses we acquire. Our aspiration should be to take each day and see its beauty beyond the things we purchase. Whether it is our spouse, children, or ourselves, it is imperative to see them through the lens of love first, rather than wealth. Sure, it is necessary to provide for and leave a monetary legacy for our family. I believe every parent desires to give their children more than they had in their childhood. Also, I believe every spouse should want to provide the best for their significant other. But, repeat after me, "Money does not define me." Having a vast financial portfolio cannot give you a great attitude, nor can it heal your body. Of course, money can pay for the best doctors, but even the best-paid doctors cannot "guarantee" your healing.

Do you judge yourself or feel that others judge you by your financial status? Too often, we view ourselves based on the tangible items we possess. We work harder daily to attain more than we already have, and even when we get "more," we are not completely satisfied. When we reach one financial goal, the word "enough" never comes to mind or protrudes from our lips. As a matter of fact, we begin to figure out how we can secure more. It seems to be a never-ending cycle of reaching a goal and immediately working feverishly for the next target. The rat race of trying to get all that we can never allow us to slow down so we can savor the moment or celebrate ourselves for reaching the first goal. Not only that, but it seems that we live in a perpetual flow of "never enough"!

While writing this book, I experienced an extremely stressful and scary time in my life. The issues that I faced personally were seemingly coming from every direction. My thoughts were discombobulated, and it felt like I did not have the stamina to finish what I had started. Every day seemed to bring an issue that I had to confront head-on. It was as if someone was standing behind a firing range, and my life and family were the targets. Trying to bob and weave through each situation became exhausting. I finally understood that there are times we ignore what we should be paying close attention to. Over a year ago, even though I felt good, my primary care physician stated that I was borderline hypertensive. I was in denial concerning this early diagnosis. However, my body did not agree with me and refused to remain in denial. Working a full-time job, maintaining my own business, parenting teenagers, consuming a poor diet, and getting minimal sleep and no exercise was my weekly regimen. But that same list of things was also what placed me under an undue amount of stress. My body was literally giving out, and it became painfully obvious when my blood pressure registered at 200/100 and I experienced debilitating chest pains! There seemed to be no way that I was going to make it. The asset of ME was on a downward spiral and crashing like a bad investment on the stock exchange.

Finally, I took a step back to have a matter-of-fact conversation with myself. Sometimes, the truth can hurt. But I had to decide whether I wanted to hear it or suffer the consequences of lying to myself. The first truth was that I was stressed and not doing well. The second truth was that drastic changes needed to be made and quickly. Although there were some situations where I had no control of the outcome, there were others where I did. That is when I finally realized that if I didn't consider my family and myself as my first asset, I could lose it all. So I scheduled an appointment to return to my doctor. This was a huge wake-up call, especially once I was placed on medication to reduce the risk of heart disease. Did I just say those words? Heart disease! Of course, that was devastating, but I was determined to see the value in myself and understand that I was an asset to my family. It was definitely time for a lifestyle change.

It is foolish to attain wealth and prosperity but die too soon from ignoring your health. Therefore, for me, change was inevitable. I replaced things like fried foods, soft drinks, and starches with more fruits, vegetables, and other healthy food alternatives. I also started meditating, exercising, and avoiding stressful situations, which can sometimes be difficult when you are a business owner or the father of teenagers. Just kidding about the teenagers! My new lease on life has slowly become a healing process and a realization of how valuable my life is to my family. In the same manner that I desire to have financial freedom, I wish to have freedom from medications. After some weeks of taking medication, changing my mindset, and working toward a healthier lifestyle, I can say that the asset of ME has increased drastically. Now, I am fit to handle other issues with less stress and more fortitude! I have created a holistic lifestyle where I love myself and my family enough to make wise choices.

Pressure, fear, and anxiety are silent killers that can manifest sicknesses and diseases in our bodies. But we should not allow stress to take us out without a fight. To reach financial freedom and gain financial assets, we fight hard, no matter how stressful it can be. By the same token, we must have that same determination to enjoy life with family and friends. Now that I am back on a healthier path, my focus is to prioritize what is important to me, and my family is far too important to me. Every day, when I wake up for work, my first thought is not about creating wealth; my first thought is my family. Just like in Finance, I want to protect my most valuable assets. I go to work with them in mind, not only to obtain wealth.

Just like in finance, I want to protect my assets. Working allows me to protect them from being homeless, experiencing food deprivation, and living a life beneath how they were created to live. Building my own business, clearing debt, and making wise investments allow me to leave a legacy for my children. My main focus will be on their physical safety, health, and emotional and mental well-being because they are my most valued assets.

Many of us believe that if we provide material possessions for our family, then everything is well. Sure, we need to furnish those things for ourselves and our family. But sometimes, we tend to forget the mental, emotional, and spiritual components that our loved ones and we need. As we become inundated by stuff, we often forget to pay attention to our loved ones' totality, which is not only the physical aspects. After walking through my health challenges, my thought process changed toward my family and me. Asking and truthfully answering a few questions helped me prioritize my life. Finally, I understand that money and wealth are only a fraction of what I desire to provide for my family. You can create your own list of questions, but here are just a few that I asked myself:

- How do I value myself and my family?
- Where does my family stand in my list of priorities?
- Do I show my family how valuable they are, aside from providing financial stability?

- Do they remain my greatest assets, or is attaining material assets my main focus?
- What steps can I take to show my family the value that I see within them?
- Am I willing to make any necessary changes when investing in myself and my family?
- Do I intentionally invest physically, mentally, emotionally, and spiritually in my loved ones?

Whew! Those were tough to answer in the beginning. Please do not read this book and think that I have everything right. There are still areas that I continue working to achieve. Each day, I know that I am blessed no matter what situation or circumstance comes. Of course, life can place you on a continuous rollercoaster ride. Hardships can take you in several different directions, but if we understand that our personal experience and our family's lives are the greatest assets, then climbing this financial mountain will not be as challenging. Yes, I know that this book is about tangible assets, eliminating debt, increasing your wealth, and building a business empire. But before you delve into financial assets, you have to pull yourself together physically, mentally, emotionally, and spiritually. You must understand that you and your family are the most essential assets.

Investments and creating a financial portfolio of multiple types of assets takes an extensive amount of research. It is definitely not for the faint of heart. Reaching a goal to accomplish financial independence requires comprehension, education, and networking with others in the field. No one has to be convinced to do the work to obtain their desired wealth. However, when it comes to viewing our family and ourselves as assets, we are not apt to do the work. We believe, if everyone is waking up, breathing, and having their needs supplied, then all is going well. But life requires so much more than that! Spending time with your spouse or children is an investment. Knowing what is happening in their lives is necessary. Showing love at every moment possible increases the chances that, together, you and your family will persevere through the challenges of life. What investment will you make for your family to show them that they're your greatest asset?

Is it wrong to want more? Of course not! Is it wrong to be content with what you have for a while? Absolutely not! Some of us are so busy attempting to maintain a lifestyle that allows us to be seen through the lens of those who are in an upper-echelon category that we forget to enjoy the lives we are living here and now. Unfortunately, making money has become what we do to gain a positive perception from others. Here's the question, what do you do when making the next big financial move causes you to miss out on the lives of your children or your spouse? Let me be clear, none of us will ever intentionally choose to live in poverty. But can you honestly enjoy a lavish life while watching the failure of your most important relationships? We must understand the loss and detriment that comes with sacrifice when we ignore our most precious assets. Yes, moving up in the financial world or establishing a booming business is a goal we all want to achieve. I most certainly want to! But what will it cost, or what and who are you willing to sacrifice? Will it cost your health, family, or emotional and mental stability? It does not have to cost any of those because the price is too high. You can maintain stability in every area of your life if you learn how to value your real assets (family) and balance your monetary assets.

Each day, we try to achieve the "American Dream," the dream to have an equal opportunity to accomplish prosperity and success. Though the American Dream is for everyone regardless of social status or racial class, many often feel judged or deterred. Because of social bias or racial discrimination, opportunities for prosperity and success are often not realized due to inequality. Sometimes, we are not afforded the opportunity to conquer the dream we want to achieve. It can seem as though we have no choice but to compare ourselves and others by their financial status. No longer is there a great concern about enjoying life at whatever level we are currently experiencing. We are made to feel like less than a person if we have not reached the high point of the American Dream. As a result, having enough has transitioned to wanting more, and wanting more eventually becomes never enough. Let me say that again, "...wanting more eventually becomes never enough."

We cannot depreciate or devalue our lives because we have not reached a specific financial goal or achieved our ultimate dream. Our eyes cannot only remain focused on tangible things; they must also focus on what is within us. Our worthiness or the way we view others should not only be defined by economic status. It is not fair to judge someone based exclusively on their "financial status." That is not a financial issue; that is a heart issue. We live in a society where the top one percent dictate many decisions. Those below that one percent have to simply follow along with the rules they create. Nonetheless, if you, like me, are not a part of that small one percent, it does not devalue who you are, who you were created to be, and what you can achieve in life. We can conquer the hurdles that we must jump over in life, but it begins with what you say to the person looking back at you in the mirror.

Your life may not be at the level that you desire; however, for every breath that you breathe, you are valuable. The value of your life, your spouse's life, and your children's lives cannot be determined by stocks, bonds, real estate, capital ventures, or business deals. Life's valuation has to first come from within yourself. Our lives cannot be based on our financial condition because it can change at any moment. It is my hope that, before you move forward in reading this book, you make sure that you see yourself and your family as your most important asset. Ensure that the way you think of yourself places you with a high valuation that cannot easily be sold or replaced. Though we experience satisfying and challenging situations, our lives do not go down in value like the latest stock on the New York Stock Exchange. Sure, we will have people that will come in and out of our lives, some for good reasons and some not so good. However, it does not depreciate our value, like a car that is ten years old. We are going to lose, and we are going to win. Even so, no matter what kind of situation we are in at this time, we must maintain in our hearts and minds that we are still the most significant asset, more valuable than the day before.

Tips on valuing the asset of You!

1. Do not measure or compare yourself to others.
2. Recognize that your existence on Earth means you are valuable.
3. Give your best, regardless of the situations or circumstances you face.
4. Help others, especially those that may be less fortunate than you.
5. Live every moment in the present because you cannot change the past.
6. Realize that you have a purpose and pursue it.
7. Be happy with who you are. Embrace your unique personality, style, and quirks.
8. Self-love is the ultimate compliment to you!

Applied Knowledge is Power

"Knowledge isn't power, applied knowledge is power"
—Eric Thomas, former NFL player

Have you ever felt powerless or that you lacked the strength to move forward? Unfortunately, I have been at that place where I have felt helpless. It is a feeling of not having the ability to change the course of your life or the feeling of wanting something you cannot afford. Power is a state of control or authority that many of us desire to have in our lives. Perhaps, we aspire to have influence in our corporate position, our family dynamic, or to simply have power over people. No matter which area we desire to have power in, if we do not have it, then we feel lost. Most of the time, when we hear the word *rich*, the word *powerful* follows. The rich and powerful! Seemingly, money gives clout, domination, or rule. That is the way society and some of the rules of law have been set. For instance, in the political arena, it seems that control is geared more toward the wealthy. Votes are cast by all eligible voters, irrespective of their financial, physical, or religious status. But it is the rich and powerful that often attempt to "buy" or persuade the candidate through giving or lobbying, as we have come to know it. Believe me, that is an entire book within itself; however, I will not deviate down that path. My point is that the power seems to only favor those that have financial wealth. The poor and middle class appear to be at the mercy of those who have enough money to make and break the rules. But the reality is that you can have power with or without money. Sure, that sounds strange, but power is not only about money. It is also about what you possess in your mind. Each of us can have an abundance of money. But if we do not have the mental capacity or knowledge to save or invest, we will return to "broke" in a short amount of time.

The term *power* has several synonyms like *control, dominance, authority,* and *influence*. But power is also synonymous with *ability, potential, competence,* and *capability*. Often, we do not realize that there is power in numbers. For example, when people unite in large numbers, they can change the trajectory or course of businesses. Furthermore, they can change policies and laws or help bring about a better way for all people. When used with the right intent, power can open doors for those who may need a helping hand. Power should never be used as a means to maintain control over someone in order to obtain ill-gotten gains. Regrettably, this is not always the case, especially when money is involved. That is one of my reasons for writing this book. It is my intention to give you some sense of *your* power or potential, not necessarily authority. The ability to see your capacity involves moving forward in freedom, the freedom to live financially independent and to help others.

Walking through life's experiences, I have endured the good, the bad, and the ugly. I have gained money, saved money, and lost money. I am sure I am not the only one! At some point in life, we have heard from parents, teachers, or a financial magician that we have power over our money. But how can we have control over money if we do not possess the right knowledge and understand its purpose? I know I may have some cynics who will say, "The purpose of money is to spend it!" Yes, that is true, yet spending money without knowledge, action, and purpose can send you to an early financial grave. You have the choice to allow money to define you, or you can determine how the money will work for you. We do not regularly see those that are rich flaunting their riches. However, back in the crevices of their business meetings, they are finding other ways to define how their money will work for them. Although they seem to have a better quality of life, you will not always see it splattered across the pages of social media! Have you ever seen Warren Buffet, Oprah, or Bill Gates on social media flaunting all the "things" they have acquired or "making it rain" with their money? I will give you a moment to think about it.

"Knowledge is power" is a phrase that has been attributed to Sir Francis Bacon. The phrase has been used for centuries throughout the world. Though there are variations of its meaning, simply stated, knowledge is a powerful tool for achieving any goal. Many believe that the more knowledge one can obtain, the more power or control one has over others. But what if I told you that I partly disagree with that phrase? Please do not close the book. Give me a chance to state my claim. Knowledge, indeed, brings awareness and understanding. It also provides an open gateway to learning. However, if knowledge is attained but never applied through experience, then what does it become? Awareness or understanding without utilization is fruitless. Therefore, I believe that knowledge *is* power, but its power is only displayed when the knowledge is applied. Knowledge, just like faith, requires action or practice. Otherwise, it is ineffective. Knowledge with action is full of power.

Knowledge without action remains powerless. Here's an example. Students are given instruction by their teachers during class. Throughout the years of elementary, high school, and college, information is dispersed into each student's mind. However, once the students graduate, they choose to either utilize what has been learned or allow it to lie dormant in their brains. When the knowledge is applied by performing a job (action), that action renders the power or potential to receive a paycheck! On the flip side, if there is no action with the knowledge, there is no paycheck. Which would you prefer?

We can often tell when someone is just coming into possession of a large sum of money or more money than they have ever had before. Before having financial freedom, there were no photos of cars, an apartment, or new clothes; it was all positive-thinking quotes. However, once money came into their possession, the posts changed. We can follow the paper trail on social media. Each post now displays a new car, home, clothes, vacations, or anything that they can obtain now that they have been given financial liberties. But we never see posts concerning an investment in stocks, bonds, property, or anything that will add to the money they have obtained. Because they have failed to become knowledgeable and actionable and have failed to fully understand the purpose of assets, their wealth will disappear in the blink of an eye. In the Yahoo! Finance article "Out of Luck: Lottery Winners Who Have Gone Bankrupt," writer Hannah Genig discusses how, in 2018, approximately one-third of U.S. lottery winners declared bankruptcy within a few years! How do you declare bankruptcy after winning a million dollars? What causes a person to lose their financial freedom after a few years and carelessly return to the same financial prison that they were in before?

There is this old idea that gaining money quickly will change the course of one's life. The notion is, as soon the big payday comes to my doorstep, everything is going to be all right. Sure, that sounds good to the ears, but unfortunately, it is a myth that we have told ourselves over and over again. Obtaining money quickly can resolve some financial issues; however, that will only happen if knowledge is gained and applied to this new financial position. You want money because you desire to have power. And you also wish to control without knowledge. You long for authority without understanding everything that comes along with it. Power with money only accentuates who you were before having money. Let me explain a little bit more. If you were addicted to drugs when you were broke, without help, a changed mind, and applying what you learned, you will simply become a wealthy drug addict. As Lynne Twist wrote in *The Soul of Money*: "If you have character flaws or blind spots, a lot of money just amplifies them."

Most of us did not grow up with a silver spoon in our mouths. Some of our families probably experienced some very disparaging times. So, if you obtain money without knowledge, action, and discipline, you will buy everything your heart desires, whether it appreciates or depreciates. It is the lottery winner syndrome, and it happens to many of us because we want to fill the void that the lack of money caused in most of our lives. However, I ask, before you go on a spending spree, can you gain power through knowledge and action along with discipline?

Practically, all of my life, I have worked hard for every penny I have received. From the age of fourteen years old to the present time, I have worked. My first job was cleaning for a furniture rental company. At the age of sixteen, I was hired as a cashier at Burger King. Because of my mother's wisdom and my desire to possess money, working has never been an issue. Now, in my adult life, I am one of the working class that wakes up, goes to work, goes home, and goes to sleep until the next day…repeat. The idea of working for a company until retirement age was etched into my thought process. Just like many Americans, I anticipate that the job I am giving my time and talent to will, one day, give back to me once I retire. But companies are quickly downsizing, and people are being replaced by robots. We have now been slapped with the harsh reality that remaining on one job until retirement may not be a reality for many us. We have all seen or heard about company lay-offs, downsizing, and closures. Often these situations send us into a tailspin, wondering how long it will be before it is our last day or last check. Unfortunately, most of us are not prepared if that does happen. Perhaps it is because we live from paycheck to paycheck while trying to keep a roof over our family's heads. Therefore, it is difficult to find the time to figure out how to find another path to financial independence.

On the flip side, some are too scared to make that first step. Several of us have knowledge but no action. This is why I state, knowledge plus action is power. Upon graduating from high school, I enlisted in the U.S. Navy. After serving my time in the Navy, I did not have any clarity on which direction my life was going. But after some time, I decided to pursue a vocation in the medical field as a nursing assistant while attending college full-time to gain a degree as a registered nurse. During my sophomore year, it dawned on me that I was headed in the wrong direction. Neither school nor nursing was my passion, nor did I believe it would lead me down the path of achieving financial gain. I was desperate to find a vocation that would support my desired lifestyle. I was not even sure what my passion was, but I knew I did not want to experience the same lack I had during my childhood. Finally, I went in another direction where I believed I could attain wealth or, at least, save enough to invest, so I could become wealthy. My decision was to obtain a CDL license as a truck driver, which has sustained me over the years. However, that was not enough for me; I did not want to settle into the realm of just enough. It has always been my desire to go beyond what I even imagined I could achieve. Fear and, sometimes, change is a scary place to be, but for me, settling for only a small portion of what life could bring was an even scarier place.

> *"There is no passion to be found playing small —
> in settling for a life that is less than the one you are capable of living."*
> —Nelson Mandela

Something deep within urged me to rise to my highest potential, something yet to be discovered. Learning new information is what I love to do, but not just any information. I absorb information that sparks my passion or gives me an unction to want to learn more. When bombarded with life's responsibilities, it is often difficult to discern what you were born to do. But through prayer, God has a way of moving us into the purpose that we were created to achieve.

I have various interests, but not all of my interests are my passions. I research almost everything that is thought-provoking to me. Many learn from listening to classroom instruction, but I learn best by literally seeing the system of what is being taught. I do not want to waste precious time studying information just for the sake of having information. I desire to gain knowledge that can be applied, not only for me but for others as well. It was not until I immersed myself in learning about wealth accumulation and investments that I discovered my passion. Sure, the training was meant to help me improve my finances. But my desire is to also help change the financial course for someone who desires stability but does not have the resources to take a course or join a networking group. As the African-American proverb that originated during slavery states, "Each one must teach one."

Over the years, I have become enthralled with everything under the topic of finance. Through the looking glass of others who have learned and succeeded in this area, my mind has been overwhelmed with information that would catapult me to financial success. Entrepreneurship, investments, and finance are just some of the topics that caught my attention. My mind became a sponge, ready to absorb information once I discovered my passion. Meeting people through financial networking events, watching finance videos on YouTube, reading articles and books, as well as researching any information concerning assets, wealth, and entrepreneurship on Google became my second breath. The knowledge I have gained through those avenues is my ticket to change the trajectory of my own financial life. With this knowledge, the doors to financial freedom opened, and I did not miss the opportunity to walk through them.

Applying what I have learned has given me an immense amount of great experiences. One of the most important things that I have learned is that using knowledge and seeing the results takes time and patience. Never attempt to rush the process or gain so much information that you become overwhelmed and are unable or unwilling to use it. Here are questions that you should ponder and answer truthfully:

1. What do you do when you have acquired information but don't believe you have enough funds to put the knowledge into action?
2. What is holding you back from taking the first step toward your passion?
3. Do you have a fear of failure or a fear of success?
4. Are you applying the knowledge you have attained, or are you allowing it to remain dormant in your brain?

Knowledge mixed with fear and inaction renders you ineffective. Yes, all of the knowledge gained is impeccable. But if it is not applied knowledge, then the only thing you will do is fill your mind with learning and no experience. Studying and learning information is excellent and definitely a step in the right direction. However, having a great deal of knowledge and keeping it stored in your cerebrum is not enough. It yields no power and definitely no prosperity! I used to think, "Why would God allow us to gain this wisdom and not use it?" We were not created to live in poverty, nor were we created to be stingy with what God gives us. And, we were not designed or set up to become failures. Yes, some ideas or experiences may fail, but that does not define us as failures. Each day we awaken, we are given a chance to gain wisdom, put wisdom into action, and live a fulfilled life.

One thing that we must understand is that our state of mind has to change. The way we see ourselves has to change. We can no longer live the status quo life of waking up, working for what we cannot afford, allowing debt to destroy our credit report, and going to sleep without peace. It is our God-given purpose to live every aspect of our lives abundantly. Fear cannot rule our lives, and lack cannot set up residence as our landlord. The wisdom that God pours into us must be put into action. Then, we will receive power. This power must not be used to tear others down; instead, it should create a way to teach or help someone else. The ultimate goal is to have the power to move from poverty to prosperity on purpose!

"There are many roads to prosperity, but one must be taken. Inaction leads nowhere." —Robert Zoellick

The Credit Card Craze

Sometimes, when we reach a certain level of financial comfort, we tend to relax our minds toward how we spend and save. Our concentration shifts from poverty to prosperity. Money allows us to hear the screams of credit card companies and big business banks. The minute we begin to pay attention, our financial peace is in jeopardy of being snatched away. We have been taught that credit cards, beautiful homes and cars, and designer clothes prove we are successful and have achieved the American Dream. But no one explains that most of those items depreciate or will cost extra if not paid back on time! We have been bamboozled and hoodwinked by our state of mind concerning money. Unfortunately, our thought process has set us on a path that will eventually lead us into a debt-driven state of mind instead of an asset state of mind. Don't worry. You are not alone. I have been there, too. But before we arrive at the street called Bankrupt or face the legal loan sharks, I simply want to share my story.

Credit, credit, credit! All you need is credit! These are the words that we consistently hear. We have been told time and time again that excellent credit is a necessity, and I agree wholeheartedly! Maintaining a good credit score grants you the ability to achieve some of the things you desire. Renting an apartment, purchasing a home, and having the working capital to run your business are some of the things that require good credit. In this section, we will not spend a great deal of time talking about good credit as it pertains to your credit score. The credit we will be discussing is the credit card craze. During this portion of the book, I am asking you to be open to the information I will share. Some of you will agree, and others of you may disagree. Often, when you hear or read about credit cards, it is from a mythical legend that we have carried throughout history. In this chapter, I want to put that mythical legend out of its misery. So let's talk about the credit craze.

The credit craze has become a phenomenon that has hit the circuit like Chubby Checkers' dance craze called "the Twist" back in the day. Everyone has the need or desire to jump in and try to be a part of this credit trend. I call it a trend because having a credit card has become a movement. People view you differently when you have a credit card. It doesn't matter whether you have available funds on it when you first walk to the cash register. All you have to do is have one, and you are deemed worthy. Though you are not the credit-card trendsetter, you are a part of an elite group. This group has defied the odds by having a good enough credit score to qualify for the almighty credit card. The feelings you have when you can pull that card from your wallet or purse can send an exhilarating chill down your spine. Your head is held a little higher because you can get the product or service you desire immediately and pay for it later. Well, you are absolutely right... you *will* pay for it later. And the later you repay, the more you will pay. That beautiful blouse charged at $39.00 or that new set of tools charged at $149.00 will soon tack on interest and fees if not paid off immediately. For those who, like Wilma Flintstone used to say back in the day, "charge it," eventually they will find themselves regretting those words and the activities that follow. Yes, some can afford to pay the charges in the same month, but most would not have charged it if the money were available at the time of purchase. Now, many find themselves in debt, worried about how the bill will get paid, and continuing to charge just to stay afloat. Which place are you in?

You have now entered the credit daze. Your head is spinning from struggling to keep up the appearance of creditworthiness while at the same time avoiding every call from debt collectors. If this describes you, then being in bondage from the high price of "charge it" has placed you in a financial prison. No longer do you walk into a store or bank with the financial peace you once had. No longer do you enjoy answering your phone if, by chance, it's from an unknown number. Checking your credit score is absolutely out of the question. The looming feeling of credit card debt has placed a dark cloud over your head. There seems to be no escape. It seems debt collectors who do not know or care about you personally only associate you with the amount of your debt. Ultimately, their job is to tell you what to do with your finances, so their client (the credit card company) can receive their money with interest. They have been assigned as your financial warden or your correctional money officer. You do not own all of your money anymore. Instead, the credit card company or debt collector informs you how much to pay, when, and where to submit payment. And if, by chance, you choose not to conform, additional fees will be added. Without hesitation, you are thrown into financial solitary confinement.

No one likes prison because it is a place of bondage, loneliness, and strict rules. This is even the case financially. Our culture has bought into the rhetoric that credit cards are our best friends and will not get us into any trouble. Please do not misunderstand; it is good to have, at least one credit card for business or emergency purposes only. But once the card becomes the "go-to" for purchases and quick fixes, you must be ready to face what comes along with it once the charges become consistent and the payments become inconsistent.

Again, knowledge without action will render you powerless. Our financial power becomes depleted when we have an overabundance of debt. Deep within the fibers of our beings, we know that the overuse of credit cards can place us in a predicament that can be life-changing for an extensive amount of time. Nonetheless, once we have acquired the credit card, what we know seems to creep out of our minds. We know that credit cards should only be utilized in situations where the amounts can be paid back immediately. Instead, we choose to swipe or insert the chip of our card at any gratifying moment. We don't consider "delayed gratification." What is delayed gratification? Simply put, it is when one resists immediate indulgence, pleasure, or satisfaction. It involves something that many of us find difficult to do… waiting. Delayed gratification is not the plague, and we should not run from it. As a matter of fact, delaying may eventually present something better.

Remember the beautiful blouse and the new tools? They may actually be placed on sale after just a week of waiting!

The only way I can share this information with you is because I have been in the financial prison of credit card debt. Having to see credit card bills every month and knowing that my minimum payments were not even scratching the surface was excruciatingly heartbreaking. Every time my wife and I wanted to have a date night or simply take a vacation, I was haunted by the fact that the amount owed on our credit card wouldn't allow us to do those things. It appeared that I was backed into a corner. But I remembered the financial research I had done, as well as the books I had read and the videos I had watched by business experts. Before the world of Google and YouTube, I read books. Yes, they were actual books, not electronic books. I read books such as *The Millionaire Next Door* by Thomas J. Stanley and William D. Danko, and *Rich Dad, Poor Dad* by Robert Kiyosaki. Also, I studied entrepreneurs like Bob Johnson, the founder of Black Entertainment Television (BET), Oprah Winfrey, and the late Dr. Myles Munroe, a prominent pastor and teacher.

As I began to recount, understand, and put into action the information I read or listened to, my state of mind changed. I was not backed into a corner. Finally, my mindset was changed to understand that there is always a way out; however, it required me to make sacrifices and experience lots of delayed gratification. Delayed gratification is okay for a few days or weeks, but when the delay turns into years, then it is difficult to maintain. Of course, when I first began denying myself the things that I desired, it was not easy, but I knew it would eventually be worth it. It took focusing on the goal and the end result.

The day my wife and I married was one of the happiest of my life. Knowing that I would spend the rest of my life with her was great. But I also knew that getting married placed the responsibility to take care of her on me. My commitment was to be a good husband and father. Remembering how hard my mother had worked to care for my siblings and me gave me the determination to make sure I cared for my family. Because they were important to me, it was vital for me to lead them in the direction of prosperity, not poverty. Though we were not living a *Lifestyles of the Rich and Famous* type of life, we were not destitute. Before getting married, we did not have enormous debt. Our responsibilities included mortgage, utilities, a car payment, three credit cards, and a few miscellaneous expenses. We financed our wedding by using two credit cards. Unfortunately, I had not considered the future impact that the debt would have on our lives. Although we briefly discussed using credit cards for the wedding and the possible implications, we were overly excited about creating a beautiful occasion. Therefore, the decision was made to use credit cards. Immediately following the marriage, we discovered we were not ready for the payments, along with the interest we were required to repay. It didn't create any disagreements between us; however, we both knew that we could not live in this financial prison of paying off our wedding for the next ten years!

The interest rates on the credit cards were low and high. Even though we did not overextend ourselves by charging the maximum amount on either of the cards, we still owed on each of them. We were reminded of the saying that we had "more bills than money." It was never my desire to make my wife unhappy. As her husband, I desired to bring a smile to her face, protect her, and make certain she had the things she needed and wanted. Yet, with debt from the credit cards, I couldn't live up to that desire. So I knew there had to be a radical change that would possibly create even more unhappiness. For me to provide for my wife the way I wanted, I needed to free up more money instead of giving it away to credit card companies. No, my wife is not overly materialistic; she doesn't ask for the world. But because of my love for her, I wanted to make sure that I could provide for her if she ever needed or wanted anything. Not only that, but it also was never in my heart to leave her in debt if something happened to me through sickness or death. I had to make it better.

Before date-night dinners, expensive vacations, new cars, or a new house, I decided to start clearing out debt in the areas where I could be most successful. Although we had several credit cards, the interest rates were different. I remembered the cliché, "the only way to eat an elephant is one bite at a time." Therefore, I began listing all my credit cards with the amounts and interest rates because you cannot fix what you do not face. Viewing the total of every card and its rates gave me a perspective on how much money was owed. Even though my wife and I agreed to tackle this debt, we both knew that we did not have a great deal of extra money. There had to be a change, not only in our state of mind but in our everyday living.

The changes to our lifestyle were challenging and, at times, placed us in an unwelcoming environment with one another. But we had to stay the course. I am not a financial wizard or a mathematical genius. Still, I had gained enough knowledge to put it into action. After writing down the card amounts and the interest rates, I began to calculate how much extra money was needed to be included with the minimum payment. We started our "credit card debt depletion" journey by paying off the credit cards with the smallest amount and least interest owed. The plan to pay off the credit cards was hard work, but I have never been a person who was afraid to work as much as needed. If it meant overtime or another job, I was up for the challenge. That is what my mother imparted to me. So to get additional funds to pay the credit cards, I worked overtime during my full-time job and took another job to generate more income. It would have been great to take a vacation with the extra money, but that was not the plan. Instead, I saved the extra money for about two or three months. During the months of saving, I continued to make the minimum payments on each card. There was never a missed payment. Finally, after saving the extra money over several months, I had enough money to pay off one of the credit cards in its entirety. I cannot explain the load that was lifted off my shoulders when that card was paid off, but even though it felt great to pay off that card, I knew that I was not done. We were ecstatic after the card was paid in full! No, there was no big celebration; it was simply thought of as a "good job" because we knew there were more cards to pay off. So I began the process all over again.

Again, putting my knowledge into action, the credit card with the highest interest rate was rolled over to a credit union-approved card with zero interest. The card came with an agreement to pay off the total amount within a set timeframe. This required sacrifice and more overtime hours at work! With each payment, we watched our credit card debt begin to disappear. Yes, it took some time, but we could breathe a little bit better with each payment. We were breaking out of the financial prison where we were being told what to do by the money guards called debt collectors. As soon as each credit card was paid in full, we canceled the card and closed the account. We were determined not to return to that place of bondage. The only thing we maintained was one credit card for business and credit purposes. However, that card remained at a zero balance unless we needed to use it for an emergency. Eliminating credit card debt gave us a sense of empowerment over our finances. Not only that, but we have also now created an accessible income that will be used for investment purposes.

If it can happen for us, it can happen for you. But first, it takes changing your state of mind and facing what you need to fix. It will take discipline, sacrifice, and maybe some overtime hours at work. But it is possible! So here's your first exercise.

1. Count the number of credit cards you have. If you are married, count the number of credit cards between you and your spouse.
2. Now, divide your cards into two groups,
    a. Cards with a balance, and
    b. Cards without a balance.
3. List the total owed for all cards.
4. List the total amount of your minimum payments for all cards.
5. List the average APR for all cards.

Often, it helps to have a visual of what we are spending. Remember, you cannot fix a problem if you do not truthfully face the problem. Here's an example, imagine you have four credit cards with a balance totaling $5,000.00 (Yes, I know that is extremely low for some of you). Let's say that each card has a balance of $1,250.00, and the average APR is 17.99%. The monthly interest amount for each credit card is $18.74. Sure, that doesn't sound like a great deal of money. But annually, an extra $224.88 will be added to each card. You will pay $674.64 per credit card in three years, without receiving any other goods or services for that amount. Think about the amount of money you could have saved or invested from the interest alone!

The credit card craze has overtaken our lives without much to show for what we are paying for. Many of us could have paid off our debts long ago. But because we lack knowledge, discipline, or action, we are stuck in the rut of making minimum payments and adding interest. The original cost of what we purchased has doubled or tripled over the years, yet we continue to charge. Instead of charging our credit, we must begin to take charge of our monetary well-being. The moment you decide to dig from the grave of debt, then the transition of power moves from the credit card company back to your home and family. Indeed, it may take some time, but with each payment, you will see the light at the end of the tunnel. Discipline is a crucial method to end credit card debt. One credit card with zero or low interest will suffice. This is not the credit card used for "feel good" purchases; it is for emergency purposes only. For two or more credit cards, only maintain the low-interest card for the same reason. Cut the rest and close the accounts. Are you ready to free up some more money? Then, let's go…

Bad Debt or Investment?

"Debt is the worst poverty." —Thomas Fuller

Financial stability and wealth management are two areas where I aspire to have great success. I haven't made this my goal to be braggadocious or arrogant. I've made this my goal so I can care for my family, leave a legacy, and pay it forward. I believe that Heaven is absolutely mind-blowing; therefore, I desire to experience a little of Heaven on earth. Some of our wealthiest one percent seem to be unaffected by some of the atrocities that take place in our country. On the other hand, some do care and have created or given abundantly to charitable organizations. That is the balance that we must learn and maintain when we get to a place of wealth or monetary increase.

*"Success isn't about how much money you make;
it's about the difference you make in people's lives."*
—Michelle Obama, from *The Legacy of Michelle Obama*

For me, having the wherewithal to invest and gain financial freedom is extremely important. Just like millions of Americans, I have experienced the pressures of debt. But what we must understand is that there are two types of debt, good and bad. You are probably wondering, How can debt be good? Well, good debt consists of those items that will eventually grow, thereby increasing your capital or long-term income. All debt does not place you in poverty unless you make extremely poor investment decisions. Good debt such as student loans, home mortgages, or financial investments come with an increase in value. For instance, obtaining a student loan can be beneficial because the educational background potentially raises your value to an employer, as well as generates a prospective income.

In the previous chapter, we covered quite a bit concerning debt. While we will continue talking about debt, we are going to talk about "intentional" good debt that can turn into bad debt. As before, allow me to explain what I mean by "intentional" good debt. When we embark on obtaining a credit card, purchasing a home, or getting a student loan, we have good intentions. It is never our intent to go into debt and settle there. That would be the definition of insanity! We understand that bad debt can consist of credit cards with exorbitant payments, payday loans with high-interest rates, or quick loans with astronomical rates. Bad debt is a vicious enemy. Over time, it will follow you like you are its identical twin. This type of debt is the one thing that can make the strongest man weak. It removes the freedom that we always dreamed of maintaining in our lives. Debt has become our slave master. It does not allow us to breathe the mental, physical, or financial freedoms we should experience. Obtaining too much bad debt causes a stressful life if left unpaid. Though attaining quick loans to fulfill your needs or wants seems like a great idea, it is not. At some point in time, payday loans will overwhelm the essence of your life to the tune of 400% interest. Bad debt is a perpetrator, masking itself as a way to get ahead of the game, but in actuality, you will be left behind.

Have you ever dreamed of doing what you love? Can you imagine not waking up just to work to pay bills but to do something that brings you peace and joy? Some of us are faced with waking up every morning or evening to prepare for a job that doesn't utilize the skills or abilities we possess. Though many of us have been employed with the same company or organization for years, we are not satisfied with the day-to-day functions we were hired to perform. It becomes something we merely do for the sake of trying to control the free fall of debt we have spiraled into. We are no longer able to enjoy life; instead, we work to escape the chokehold of debt. Years and years of debt have overtaken many of us, and it often happens gradually. Usually, money owed begins because we believe that we will have the resources to repay the debt quickly. College loans are considered good debt but can quickly become bad debt because the career we were prepared for is not readily available. For instance, college students take out student loans for the number of years they attend school. The hope is to receive their degree, start a great-paying job in their field, and begin repaying the debt. However, proven by the amount of debt owed for student loans (over $1 trillion), we understand that having the resources to quickly repay the debt does not always happen. Millions of Americans are drowning in student loan debt. This debt has become so unbearable that even politicians are trying to find a way to totally cancel it and reduce the cost of college to free!

Good debt, such as student loans or home mortgages, is not a bad thing to have. However, we must remember that if payments are inconsistent, good debt will turn into bad debt and negatively impact our lives. Many people, myself included, have multiple sources of income, but bad debt seems to try to continuously take over our lives. Here's what I have learned. Instead of allowing financial deficiencies to become an intrusion, we must remove those deficiencies from our lives as quickly as possible. But that takes work! Until we make conscious decisions, ultimate sacrifices, and a substantial commitment to eliminate debt, then we will never experience financial freedom. Once we begin to walk a path toward removing negative debt from our business portfolio, then we will see the trajectory of our finances shift to prosperity.

> *"If you buy things you do not need,
> soon you will have to sell things you need."*
> —Warren Buffet

What is holding you back from the financial freedom that you desire to experience? How can you avoid letting debt impede your life until it ultimately sends you into an economic rollercoaster, which leaves you up, down, and upside down? Besides your family, what is the priority in your life? These are the questions that I had to ask myself. Not only was it essential for me to ask myself these questions, but it was equally important to answer them truthfully. Facing yourself in the mirror about decisions you have or have not made is often a daunting task. We do not see the business loan as a debt; we only see the money that can help with our start-up. Don't get me wrong.

Obtaining business loans is not a bad thing. However, the repayment of that loan when the business does not accumulate money in the time specified by the repayment contract must be thought about and prepared for. For most of us, it is never our intention to remain in debt. Financial freedom is achievable, but getting there often sends us into disparity or causes us to make desperate decisions that can drive us into more debt. The unfortunate part is that being on a financial rollercoaster places a heavy burden on our relationships, health, and mental stability. It can lead to divorce, depression, and other decisions that can guide us into creating more debt.

Life happens, circumstances change, and resources become depleted. So what do you do when your debt seemingly places you in an uncontrollable situation? How do you handle becoming debt-free? Again, be realistic about your debt. Write it down. Look at it. This is not a time for pride, embarrassment, or shame to come to the forefront. Overcoming insurmountable debt has to be alleviated, like losing weight, one pound at a time. I must admit, clearing out debt is one of the hardest things to do because it takes discipline. But when you get to the point in life where debt is overtaking every part of your life, then it is time to do something about it.

Like any other person, I don't like debt or owing on something that will yield no return. I prefer economic freedom. It came to a point where I was tired of working to pay someone else. The money that I worked hard to accumulate was instantly given to someone that only gave me a portion of what I was paying back. On the road of debt, I could work hard but could never play hard. The repetitive cycle of wake up, go to work, and sleep; without having any memories of truly living life significantly impacted my family and me. Our mortgage balance was within reach of a zero balance. Therefore, my goal was to reach a mortgage balance of zero and an increase in living life abundantly.

Here's my story of getting off the rollercoaster. A couple of years ago, I decided to be more proactive at becoming debt-free. After clearing the credit card debt, my wife and I knew that the mortgage was another one of the most significant obligations we wanted to do away with. Although the mortgage was consistently paid every month, more funds were geared toward the interest than the principal. Through research, I learned that banks have a higher interest rate when the loan amounts are more. However, as the loans decrease, the interest rates also decrease. It became apparent that if we wanted to erase this chunk of debt, we had to pay more toward the principal. Our home was under a fifteen-year mortgage loan. Although a thirty-year loan seemed favorable because of the lower payments, I knew that we would pay more in interest over time. Therefore, we opted for a fifteen-year with a fixed interest rate. Utilizing the information concerning the interest amounts charged by banks to consumers, I created a budget to completely eliminate the fifteen-year mortgage. I realized that paying lump sums toward the principle drastically reduced the amount owed. Since there were extra funds from paying the credit card debt, I consistently paid an extra two to three times our mortgage. Each extra payment was specified to be applied directly toward the principle of the loan. Of course, I wish I could tell you that it was the easiest thing to do every month, but it was not. You would think it was easier because we had done it before with the credit cards. However, the higher the amount, the harder it is to let go of the extra money. Paying off the mortgage seemed to be an even greater sacrifice to my wife and me, but we were determined to keep the goal in mind and our eyes on the finished line. After a year of consistent payments on the principal, the final payment was made! I cannot explain every feeling I had as I walked into the bank, but I knew this would free up funds for other investments and give my wife a well-deserved vacation, and that I was excited about.

No, everyone cannot afford to pay an extra two to three times their mortgage. However, if you have any extra money, say $50 or $100, then pay it toward the principal. Because we see the $1,200.00 mortgage payment, we may feel that the extra $50 will not help, but it will. If you pay $50 per month, then at the end of the year, you have decreased your principle by $600.00. You will never know if it works until you try. Commitment, patience, discipline, hard work, knowledge, and action are some of the words you will need to repeat when you are ready to eradicate your debt. Whether it is good or bad debt, we cannot allow it to become the one-eyed monster that takes over our lives. Time and again, we become so overwhelmed with looking at the big picture. We stare at our mountain of debt until we stop believing that we can overcome the economic or monetary challenges that we face. However, this is the time for you to make a commitment to take another bite of the elephant. Let's do an exercise.

1. Gather all of the utility bills, additional loans, and first or second mortgages in one area.
2. Place them in order from the least to the highest amount owed.
3. Review your minimum payments.
4. Record the information in a journal.
5. Research and gain clarity on your home loan interest rate; you may qualify for refinancing with a lower interest rate.
6. Speak with your lender to negotiate payment amounts or payoff balances.
7. Assess what you can commit to sacrifice (i.e., eating out for lunch or dinner, extracurricular activities, high-dollar purchases).
8. Figure out how long it will take to pay off the debt by making an extra payment.
9. Schedule the timeline you would like to pay off the debt by.
10. Take the extra money (we'll call this "future investment money") and apply it to the debt with the least amount owed.
11. Stay focused and committed.

Maybe you cannot pay an extra $1,000.00 toward the principle or even an additional $50 toward your credit card bill. However, you must be honest about your commitment to purge your debt. What do I mean? As my wife and I endeavored to eliminate the mortgage on our home, it took a considerable amount of commitment. Sacrificing some of the things that would give us immediate gratification was not the easiest thing to do. That meant giving up doing some pleasurable ventures and putting a hold on purchasing high-priced items. The same way getting rid of credit card debt did not create a comfortable home environment; neither did wiping out the mortgage. But during the process, we further realized that communication, commitment, and unity are the keys to reaching the goal. These principles and sacrifices are the same, whether you are married or single. Excluding bad debt or good debt that has overextended its stay opens the door to doing the things you have only dreamed of. It is not an unattainable dream that only the rich can achieve. You can reach your goal, but it depends on you. Each day, you must commit, communicate, and execute delayed gratification. Although we have utilized the term *sacrifice* when delaying some of the things we desire, ultimately, they are investments.

> *"Some of your activities should be viewed as an investment and not a sacrifice."* —Anonymous

The Door to Entrepreneurship

Many Americans are suffering financially, but we don't have to remain in a state of lack. Poverty or having just enough resources was not the plan for your life. I understand that life's tragedies have been the cause of where you are financially. None of us have a crystal ball to see the future, nor can we unplan those hardships that come out of nowhere. When you are faced with continuous atrocities, it can take your breath away and send you into a tailspin of negativity. Nonetheless, you can make it through. Is it difficult? Absolutely! Is it possible? Absolutely! It depends on you and your mindset.

Your life requires you to "think" beyond what you are facing. A changed mind and determination are pivotal to changing the course of your life. In like manner, the same requirements are needed to reach your financial goals. Achieving economic wealth requires you to change your mind, to change how you "see" money. Your mental state controls a significant part of your life. Therefore, how you think determines the direction of your life. Even when you hit a rough financial patch in life, the way you think and respond to the situation controls the outcome. Sure, you can become defeated, but you can also become victorious. Throughout this book, the ultimate message is about changing your mind. Once you've done that, then you can walk the path to experiencing financial stability and wealth. However, if you wish to continue on the road that you are walking with the thought of "I wish," then that is your choice. But it doesn't have to be that way.

Entrepreneurship is a word that many of us have heard; unfortunately, many of us do not believe we can possess our own businesses. We were all born to fulfill a purpose, but some do not know their purpose and have settled in a place of safety. Though many of us desire to become financially stable and function in our own niche, there is no urge to move in that direction by becoming an entrepreneur. Instead of thinking outside the box or getting rid of the box, many of us are more comfortable staying in the box. Being an entrepreneur is definitely not for the faint of heart or for those whose work ethic is not up to par. Starting and managing a business takes long days and nights of planning, creativity, finance, and the tenacity to stand firm even when the company does not generate income immediately. I was once told, "To be an entrepreneur, you must have thick skin." In other words, you will encounter several highs and lows, so your mindset has to be intact for success. It gets tough at times, but you must remain focused. I would say, experiment until you find your niche and find a mentor who has mastered it.

> *"I think a great entrepreneur is learning every day. An entrepreneur is somebody that doesn't take no for an answer — they're going to figure something out. They also take responsibility. They don't blame anybody else. And they're dreamers in one sense, but they're also realistic, and they take affordable steps when they can."*
> —Damon John

Many shy away from starting their own businesses for several reasons. Maybe it is because there seems to be more failures than successes, or perhaps the word "no" has been heard more times than "yes." The stresses that possibly come along with becoming an entrepreneur cannot be faced chaotically or without excellent planning. As a business person, there are times that it will seem that, for every step forward, there are ten steps backward. Entrepreneurship sounds good. The word rolls off the tip of the tongue, but it takes a great deal of work. However, for those close to giving up on their dream, before you throw in the towel, consider fulfilling your purpose one more time. I understand the conversations that you mull over and over in your mind. We often stop trying because we may not have the finances to begin, and the current business plan is a blank sheet of paper that taunts you every time you look at it. Fear plays a role in not moving forward; therefore, you make the decision to maintain your full-time job because, at least, it gives you a way to pay your bills. Although you may be living paycheck to paycheck, you are happy that you are not living in your car. I get it! But moving out of your comfort zone to work on that dream is not as daunting as it seems. By the way, who says that you must immediately quit your full-time job to start your own business. If the full-time job helps you to fund your dream, then don't walk away.

What do you want out of life? What are you willing to sacrifice to reach your goal? Will you put in the work, no matter how long it takes? As I have read and studied the advice of some of the best financial gurus and those that have done well in business, I've realized that it takes time, research, moving out of your comfort zone, and tenacity. Starting your business may require you to return to school, network with others who run similar companies, and take risks. Entrepreneurs will take a chance because they understand that they must figure out what will work and what will not work. Though every business does not require a hefty amount of money, it does require some start-up funds. Starting a business requires you to change your spending habits and implement delayed gratification. The time to gain your life back from the pit of poverty and debt is now. Use your income as a wealth-building tool. It's about creating the life of your dreams and leaving a legacy for future generations. Renew your mindset for a lifestyle makeover. It all starts with you!

> *"It's not how much money you make,*
> *but how much money you keep, how hard it works for you,*
> *and how many generations you keep it for."* —Robert Kiyosaki

Often, we dive into corporate America to work extremely hard for our money, but we are too tired to see where it is going and how we are spending it. We find ourselves trapped in the same job for twenty-five years with little to no retirement or pension. Moreover, we find ourselves having to work even harder in our latter years. Some of us were brought up to believe that if you work at a company for over twenty-five years, then you will be set for life. But we find ourselves working all those years and having nothing tangible to show for it. Sure, the house is almost paid off, the children are out of college, and we own our cars. But what else? Even after the twenty-five-year job sentence, you are still trying to dig your way out of your personal financial ditch. It seems like you will never get ahead of this economic game. Your money never seems to be working for you; instead, you are steadily working for it.

One thing I have learned from some of the wealthiest people on this planet is that they invest in products and people that will earn them money, even when they are asleep. They are seasoned entrepreneurs. Not only do they invest through stocks, bonds, and real estate property, but they also invest in their own creativity. The gift or talent they possess is what they utilize to create another form of investment. Sure, they started from somewhere, and many times, they may have started from the bottom. However, because of their perseverance and ability to tap into their inner strengths, they attain their goal of entrepreneurship. Becoming an entrepreneur is not something you achieve overnight. It takes education, a business plan, finances, and a heart to work more than anyone else affiliated with your business. However, once you reach the level of success you desire, then you will reap the benefits, even while you are asleep. My mother always told me, "Never put all your eggs in one basket." I realized I needed more than one income to live on my terms. As Warren Buffett said, "If you don't find a way to make money while you sleep, you will work until you die." That statement alone provoked me to gain multiple income-generating assets. My goal is to make money and maintain wealth when I am awake and when I am asleep, and one income will not help me reach that goal.

Working has never been difficult for me. Since the ripe age of fourteen, I have worked steadily. Sheer determination is what drove me to work for what I desired. As I stated before, my first experience in the workforce was when I walked into a furniture rental store and negotiated for a store cleaner position. For a fee, I cleaned their store every week. Because of my quick learning, work ethic, and determination, I was promoted to store operations over a short amount of time. The manager trusted me with additional responsibilities, including learning how to operate the store, assist customers, and manage customer accounts. This was a valuable, first-hand experience for a kid who had the sheer ambition to succeed in making their own money. My job at Burger King was also a good learning lesson. The customer service training acquired through this position was a valuable asset that would be needed later as an entrepreneur. From each job, I gained transferrable skills that would prepare me for my next career move and, ultimately, my own business. Being employed did not just mean having a job. I had dreams! I felt like Martin Luther King, Jr. because "I Have A Dream!" My goal was to enter into the workforce with aspirations in mind. Those goals were to learn the skills of how to run a business, customer service, technology, and any additional skillsets that were offered. There was nothing that I didn't want to learn. Of course, I wanted to earn money, but making money is not the only thing needed to maintain a business. There are several requirements to ensure a business will have longevity.

The skills I acquired working at the furniture store and at Burger King allowed me to develop into a reliable, consistent, and dependable employee. My verbal communication and customer service skills increased tremendously. After working these first two jobs, I had a clearer understanding of the expectations that came with working in corporate America. I will not say that there have not been challenging experiences while working, especially with customers; nevertheless, I learned how to handle problematic situations. A few years after graduating from high school, I worked as a nursing assistant. Functioning in this position gave me a positive outlook on life because it was rewarding. Assisting patients and taking care of their well-being was gratifying, and the pay was considered an honest day's wage. No, I could not get rich from what I was paid, but I had just enough to pay my bills. There was little to no money left over, but I was not homeless! Although I was quite happy about not being homeless, I still did not want to live pennilessly. Plus, I wanted a business that I could call my own.

One day I thought, There must be a better way! In my environment, I was not surrounded by doctors, lawyers, politicians, or any other people in high-paying positions. I was surrounded by people such as fast-food workers, warehouse workers, and truck drivers. Most of them were barely getting by. Please don't get me wrong; there is absolutely nothing wrong with making an honest wage through any of those jobs. All I knew was that I wanted more out of my life. I was tired of doing the same thing every day and coming out with barely enough to survive. Throughout my life, I was never fascinated by luxurious items. I wanted assets that would give me cashback while I slept!

In my neighborhood, we also had people who were known as "street pharmacists" or "street hustlers." It was always amazing to me how these street hustlers had the most expensive items and had larger than life personas. It was never my intention to become one of them, but I was definitely interested in their ability to never be broke and their ability to maintain what they desired. As a result, I decided to have a conversation with one. One day I posed a question to one of the street hustlers, who always traveled with lots of cash. I asked him, "Why do you hustle the way you do?"

He replied, "You just keep playing it safe. I'll continue taking risks as an entrepreneur." That statement penetrated the core of my being. I was intrigued by his response for

many reasons. The main reason was that I wanted to control my financial destiny, but I wanted to do it legally. It was time to figure out my passion.

> *"The only link between my experience as an employee and that of an entrepreneur is all in one word: Passion."* —Nitya Prakash

If you had to decide on a dream job, what would it be? Whatever you are passionate about is your purpose on earth. People all over the world have different passions, and some are the same, but our personalities and creativity develop the difference. Our passion is really our purpose. Our purpose is God's intent for our lives. And, there is a vast difference between a purpose and a hobby. When there is a passion for doing something, there is hunger or an urge to succeed in that area. You wake up and go to sleep, thinking, planning, and putting into action how to achieve working your passion. On the other hand, a hobby is a leisure pursuit or interest in an idea or a craft. A hobby does not necessarily present those strong feelings of achieving a goal or being awakened in the middle of the night to write a business plan. Your passion brings excitement, fascination, hard work, creativity, the pursuit of more education, and the need to meet others who are experts in that area. For me, my passion is barbering. Sure, you may think that it is simple, but it requires intense work and instruction, especially to be successful.

Barbers fascinate me with their picture-perfect hairstyles. In my eyes, they are artists, and their medium of choice is hair. They create an environment full of entertainment and change lives simply by changing a hairstyle. After realizing this, I was intrigued. I decided to start a service-based business. I knew art was my passion, and I loved to watch local barbers develop their craft. They were creating amazing sculptures with hair. That was my ticket to full entrepreneurship! After working for a salon for seven years, my vision was to own a barbershop. Let's be clear, you may not always know what your passion is as you exit the womb. Sometimes, it takes watching someone else do something before you figure out what excites you and brings out your enthusiasm. Do not be ashamed if you have a late start with building your business or pursuing your passion. The main thing is that you start. Move your mindset from the negativity of "it's too late" or "everybody is already doing it." There may be several people working in the same field, but they are not YOU! Focus on your dream, your passion, your goal, and your business!

When planning your business, it can be overwhelming. Many of us do not know where to begin. It seems like such a big task, but others make it look so easy. I will repeat that famous quote again, "The only way to eat an elephant is one bite at a time." You're not in a race against anyone. It is better to take the time to build your business than to build a business that will not succeed. Every business is not the same; therefore, it may take a shorter time or a longer time to establish a successful and profitable company. The key is to persevere and stay focused. Allow me to share some of the steps I used to start my business. Since I have a family that is dependent on me to care for them, the first step was to discuss my vision and plans with them. Whether the business skyrocketed or failed, they were going to be impacted. The second step was to create a business plan, which included a business overview, market analysis, financial strategies, competition analysis, and future growth or projections. Your business plan becomes a roadmap to building your business.

Next, it was essential to establish the business through the city and state. Setting up your business correctly is essential. Ensuring your business is set up correctly can include:

- Creating a business name
- Obtaining a tax number
- Deciding between sole proprietorship or LLC
- Establishing bank accounts
- Attaining licenses, certifications, or insurances
- Purchasing a domain and email addresses for website setup (if applicable)

These are just a few items, but they are important to begin your business. Taking each of those steps for my business was quite a task. But there was still more. After making sure that the business was established on paper, it was time to search for a location within my budget. In the beginning, maintaining the flow was capital intensive (meaning it required large amounts of money), so it was important to establish a realistic budget.

Before we move on, here's a word of wisdom in case you missed it in the previous chapter. If you are unable to financially fund your business without a job in corporate America, do not quit your day job. Many immediately quit their jobs without knowing if the company will be successful or quickly turn a profit. My word to you, if you need to do both for a while, though it will be tedious and tiring, it will also be worth it!

Now let's move on. Once the location was rented, equipment was purchased to furnish the barbershop. Since my clientele had already been established, marketing and advertising were not as stressful. I officially became a business owner and a self-employed barber in 2005. Yes, I did it! While it has been a fantastic venture, it has also been eye-opening, which is why I wanted to share this information with you. My business is still growing, and I have not arrived at the level of success I desire or one that will allow me to make money while I sleep. But I will not give up on my dream. That is one of the main statements I want to say to you.

You did not pick this book up by happenstance. Of course, some of you purchased the book because you know me professionally or personally. Still, as you have read each chapter, I hope the words on these pages have pushed you to dream again. Dream of owning your business. Dream of buying residential or commercial property. Dream of becoming an investor and building your portfolio. Dream of leaving a legacy for your family. Once you see that dream in your heart, you must work every day to turn that dream into a reality.

Love Life. Make Money.

Love the life you have while you create the life of your dreams.
—Hal Elrod, bestselling author of *The Miracle Morning*

Before ending this book, allow me to share a transparent moment, along with a tidbit of encouragement. Writing and publishing this book has been a dream come true. Although it has always been my desire to share what I have learned, along the way, I had a few doubts that it would ever manifest. Plus, I figured having a conversation with a few people about financial investments, assets, and entrepreneurship was as far as I needed to go. Even after building my business, knowing my self-worth, and generating investments, writing my thoughts for you to read seemed to be a pipe dream. There are moments in life where doubt will creep in unexpectedly. Sometimes, it is because of the painful experiences, the times we may have failed, or even our age. Uncertainty seems to set in right at the moment that we get our second wind. During those times, we place our desires on the backburner. While we secretly hope that, one day, we will achieve the dream, we do not put forth a great deal of effort to make it come true. Well, this time, I decided to not only hope but to remove the barriers from my mind and make this dream come true. Sometimes, when we least expect it, a burst of energy or a simple conversation with a friend will move us to spring into action with the words of Nike™, "Just do it!" So after you finish reading this book, dust off your dreams and begin to work toward fulfilling every one of them. Of course, it may not happen overnight, but with each step, you are closer to seeing your dream come true.

The trajectory this book has taken since the initial writing has changed. At the outset of this book, my thought process was to speak only about financial wealth, investments, assets, and entrepreneurship. The intent was to share information that would help you begin the journey to fulfilling your business and economic accomplishments. While these remain the primary focus, it took a turn when I realized that our experiences will be different as we change our minds and self-worth. Life has a way of changing our perspective; sometimes, as we get older, our visions shift. We no longer see the world or ourselves through the same lens. Our experiences in life further develop our perspective concerning the path we will take. Those negative experiences should become a source of wisdom and not the foundation we are building our physical, mental, emotional, spiritual, and financial structure on.

Imagine yourself beyond what you see right now. Even if you have reached some of your goals, imagine beyond the normalcy you have become accustomed to. As you look at yourself in the mirror of life, see your worth, not from the point of arrogance, but from a position of success. From this position, you can guide someone else to their financial destiny. View every day as a new day to change the course of your life or implement something new. No, not only in the area of finance, but in how you treat your family and others, the way you go after your dreams, or the way you handle your business. You were created to be an asset, not a liability. The way you think, your perceptions, and your focus allow you to move forward with tenacity. I am aware that our past can, sometimes, be so draining that we cannot seem to shake it off, but I ask you to follow this simple advice:

- Persevere through the challenging moments.
- Believe that you can achieve your dreams.
- If needed, go to therapy, return to school, change jobs, or get an accountability partner.

Nothing in life is gained without effort. Achievement takes grit, courage, and determination. You can always shoot for the moon, but first, you must get on the space shuttle.

I am not finished with my journey. There's more information to learn, more investments to make, and more businesses to create. I am not stopping until I have emptied out all that God has given me the ability to perform. In the meantime, what I have learned and implemented has allowed me to live differently than I did before. When breaking free from the same mundane life, exciting ventures should be pursued. Clearing credit card debt, the home mortgage, and starting a flourishing business has allowed me to give my wife and family back things they sacrificed. One of the things that I was able to provide was a deserved vacation to New York City for my wife and me. Yes, we left the children!

New York is a place of bright lights, fast living, and enormous possibilities. During our stay, my wife and I were engulfed in exciting nightlife and countless activities. The flight to New York was filled with breathtaking aerial views of clouds at 30,000 feet. Upon our arrival, a cab was hailed to take us to the hotel. Gazing from the window of the cab, I was excited to take my wife on vacation. This was an exciting time where we were able to celebrate the work we had done to clear our debt. We knew there were other things that we desired to do financially. But it was this special moment that let us experience the payoff for staying true to our vision. Some may say that New York is a typical location to visit and not a big deal. Yet, for us, it was not just a location; it was the place where financial aspirations can come true, whether as an entrepreneur or a stock investor. The excitement between both of us was at an all-time high and almost led to a high-school-esque giddiness.

While traveling to the hotel, we were delighted and overwhelmed by the towering buildings, huge, vividly lit billboards, and tons of people from all over the world. Upon arrival at the hotel, we were astonished by its opulence. With immense water features, crystal chandeliers, and elevators that whisked us to dizzying heights as we ascended to our hotel room, it was a sight to behold. The room came with a deluxe view of the Empire State Building. Over the next few days, my wife and I explored the city of Manhattan for all its splendor. The tours covered numerous attractions in downtown and uptown Manhattan, such as Times Square, the Empire State Building, the Macy's building, SOHO, Chinatown, Rockefeller Center, Central Park, the Metropolitan Museum of Art, and the famous Apollo Theater, where dreams come true. One of the most exciting attractions of the tour was Wall Street. This financial district's name originated from an actual wall that was built in the seventeenth century by the Dutch, who were living in what was then called New Amsterdam. Also, in the financial district, we were able to see the bronze sculpture known as "Charging Bull," which is a symbol of market optimism. Of course, this was fascinating to me. I had read about and had heard much about this financial epicenter, so it was great to see it up close and personal.

When our trip was coming to an end, we couldn't leave without having one more significant moment. After traveling to LaGuardia Airport and while getting set to board our returning flight, we saw the incredible Phylicia Rashaad, a beautiful actress who made her mark in society. Speaking with her was an experience that touched the core of my heart. Her character on-screen exuded through her face-to-face demeanor, she is a woman of poise, grace, and humility, a queen of sophistication and class. Every moment was a fantastic experience in New York. Many come to New York in hopes of new beginnings. I returned home with a refreshed, reborn, and limitless state of mind, ready to tackle the world.

I hope that through all I have shared, you understand that this is not only concerning money, wealth, investments, or businesses. The main focus is YOU. It is imperative to know who you are. Know your value and live a life that is not riddled with arrogance and pride but humility. Do not self-sabotage because you do not believe you are worth more than your past. Your life and those surrounding you while you live on this earth are more important than having all the money in the world. Yes, it is great to have financial stability, but if you only desire to get to that point so that you can have power and control, then you must take a self-check of your character. Not only should you have an impressive financial portfolio, but you should be remarkable in every aspect of your life — physically, mentally, emotionally, and spiritually. The money will come as you learn principles and implement the knowledge you gain.

Moreover, it is essential to have the heart to help others. Leave an inheritance for your family and know that the only way to live this type of life is through God's help. Again, I will not overwhelm you with spiritual profundity, but I believe that God directs our paths and helps us live the best life we can while on earth. Our job is to make every day count. Live in the hope that we will achieve the goals we desire. Make sure our lives are beacons of light for others to see.

Now that we've talked about focusing on knowing yourself first, let's switch gears. The goals, visions, and plans you have set are attainable. I did not provide in-depth instructions with charts, graphs, and forms on how to reach your financial goals. Nonetheless, the information I shared has been tried and proven through my experience. You cannot reach the pinnacle that you desire without hard work and sacrifice. Hard work, strength, and perseverance are the keys to hitting your financial target. Don't attempt to set your goals so high that you will become discouraged when you don't reach them in a short amount of time. If you are planning to demolish your debt, start with paying extra on the highest balance. Only do an amount that will not place you in a predicament where you will create additional financial burdens. When I decided to tackle our credit card debt, it was crucial. It was necessary to look at the total amount of money coming in and the amount of money paid for other bills such as a mortgage, utilities, and other essentials. Once I had clarity on the monthly bills, then I could make a conscious decision on the amount that could be added to decrease the highest credit card.

Additionally, do your homework. Find out if you qualify for a no-interest card that will allow you to transfer your balances from other cards. In that way, you avoid the interest that is being added every month. Trust me, going through this process was not an easy feat or a quick turnaround; it took some time, but as you have read, it was well worth it. If you are married, be sure to include your spouse in these decisions. Their input is vital, and since they may be making some sacrifices, at least, allow them to see and understand the process, as well as the set objectives. Also, if you have children who are of age to understand finances, have a conversation with them regarding financial spending, saving, and investing. You never know; they could be like me and want to work at an early age to begin implementing what you are teaching them.

Society has shown us that the rich get richer and the poor get poorer, but it doesn't have to be that way. Once you climb the ladder of financial success, go back and take someone by the hand to help them climb the ladder. This book was written with that mission in mind. My next step is to create even more avenues for financial wealth. My ultimate goal is to take care of my family and myself, gain more information, implement it, and take what I know and pass it on. Your time is now! Start or continue to work toward your goals. If you have not begun the journey, don't worry, it's not too late. Don't become overwhelmed with what you see in front of you. I could only write this book one word at a time. By the same token, you will reach your goals and make your dreams come true by taking one moment at a time. I believe in you! Now, close this book and make your dreams a reality!